Pitkin County Library

What Do You Hear When Cows Sing?

And Other Silly Riddles

by Marco and Giulio Maestro
pictures by Giulio Maestro

HarperCollins*Publishers*

HarperCollins®, 🐧®, and I Can Read Book ®
are trademarks of HarperCollins Publishers Inc.

WHAT DO YOU HEAR WHEN COWS SING?
And Other Silly Riddles
Text copyright © 1996 by Marco and Giulio Maestro
Illustrations copyright © 1996 by Giulio Maestro
Printed in the U.S.A. All rights reserved.

Library of Congress Cataloging-in-Publication Data
Maestro, Marco.
    What do you hear when cows sing? And other silly riddles / by Marco
and Giulio Maestro.
        p.   cm. — (An I can read book)
    ISBN 0-06-024948-X. — ISBN 0-06-024949-8 (lib. bdg.)
    1. Riddles, Juvenile. [1. Riddles. 2. Jokes.] I. Maestro, Giulio.
II. Title. III. Series.
PN6371.5.M317   1996   94-18686
398.6—dc20   CIP
                                                                      AC

1   2   3   4   5   6   7   8   9   10

First Edition

What Do You Hear
When Cows
Sing?

What do you call a train

that sneezes?

CHOO CHOO

Ah-choo-choo train.

What kind of bug

wears a red dress?

A ladybug.

What are soft, white visitors

from Mars?

Martian-mallows.

How did the robot

wear earrings?

11

She had her gears pierced.

12

Why did the sailor

love her cookies?

They were full of chocolate ships.

What kind of bugs like toast?

Butterflies.

What did the bread

do on vacation?

17

It loafed around.

What made the mice afraid

to take a swim?

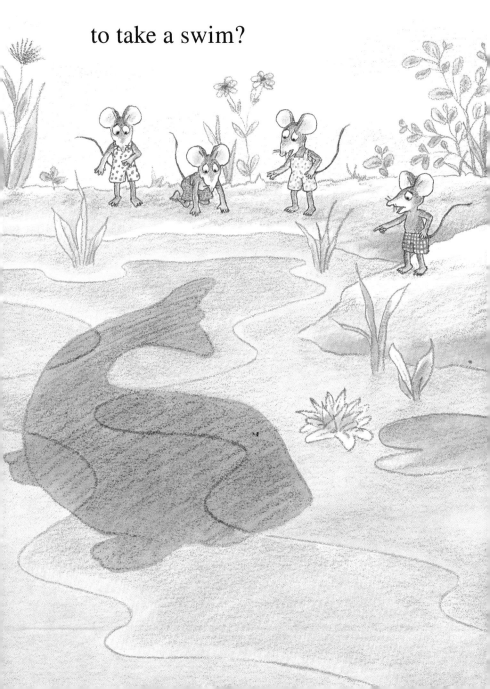

The catfish.

Why did the fish look so sharp?

She was a swordfish.

What animal is good at hitting

a baseball?

23

A bat.

What vegetable is hot

even in winter?

25

A chili pepper.

Why did the bug stay at home?

It was a housefly.

Why did the geese

honk at the piggy driver?

He was hogging the road.

What kind of snake loves

to build with blocks?

31

A boa constructor.

What kind of fish

did the miner catch?

A goldfish.

Where do aliens

keep their coffee cups?

35

On flying saucers.

What cereal do little kids
have for breakfast?

Goatmeal.

What do you hear

when cows sing?

Moosic.

Why was the insect

galloping around?

It was a horsefly.

Why were the boats

all lined up?

They were rowboats.

Why was the knight

afraid of the little insect?

It was a dragonfly.

What do you call bedtime stories

for boats?

Ferry tales.